Is It a ... ?

By Sally Cowan

Is it a ...?

Is it a pit?

Is it a mat?

Is it a tap?

It is a tap.

Pam sips at the tap.

Sip, sip, sip!

tap

It is a pit.

Mim and Sam
sit at the pit.

Pat, pat, pat!

pit

It is a mat.

Tim sits.

Sit, sit, sit!

mat

CHECKING FOR MEANING

1. Who is at the tap? *(Literal)*

2. Where are Mim and Sam? *(Literal)*

3. What do you think Tim is doing on the mat? *(Inferential)*

EXTENDING VOCABULARY

is	Look at the word *is*. What are the sounds in this word? Use *is* in a sentence to describe one of your friends.
it	Look at the word *it*. Which of these letters can be added to the front of *it* to make a new word – s, a, p?
tap	Look at the word *tap*. What letters make up this word? Can you find another word in the book that uses the same letters?

MOVING BEYOND THE TEXT

1. What are some places where you might find a drinking tap?

2. Which of the activities in the book do you like best? Why?

3. What questions would you ask Tim if you were at the gym?

4. What other guessing games do you know?

SPEED SOUNDS

| Mm | Ss | Aa | Pp | Ii | Tt |

PRACTICE WORDS

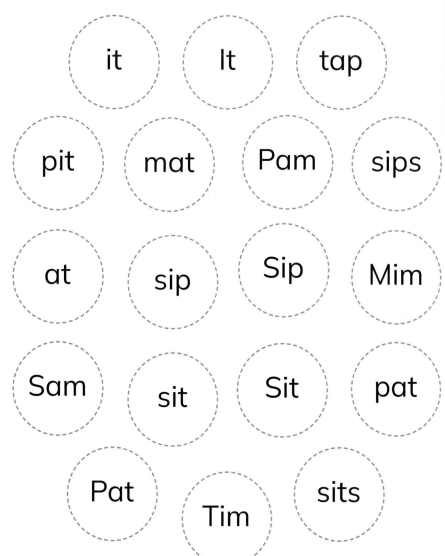

it

It

tap

pit

mat

Pam

sips

at

sip

Sip

Mim

Sam

sit

Sit

pat

Pat

Tim

sits